Thinking of...

Planning for ERP in the Cloud?

Ask the Smart Questions

By Stephen Parker

Smart Questions™ Philosophy

Smart Questions is built on 4 key pillars, which set it apart from other publishers:

1. *Smart people want Smart Questions not Dumb Answers*
2. *Domain experts are often excluded from authorship, so we are making writing a book simple and painless*
3. *The community has a great deal to contribute to enhance the content*
4. *We donate a percentage of revenue to a charity voted for by the authors and community. It is great marketing, but it is also the right thing to do*

www.Smart-Questions.com

Reviews

"This is the best description and directive on Cloud, specifically ERP Cloud, that I have read to date. In less than 80 pages, the Smart Questions book gives a really nice breakdown of Cloud descriptions and priorities which helps bring order to all the "Cloud Marketing" chaos out there in the market. I think this was a tremendous idea by Microsoft, to partner on developing this content for the "Asking the Smart Questions" series. The questions proposed are right on the money and providing simple answers to "Why it matters" helps drive clarity to my evaluation of the cloud as a business owner. I would score this content as a bull's-eye!"

Matt Woodward, President, SMB Suite

"As Partners contemplate moving their business to the cloud, it is important to go through the right thought process to determine the needs, motivation, and important business changes and challenges such a move can potentially create. Planning for ERP in the Cloud is a great guide that will help partners take a 360 degree view of the potential effect on their customers, vendors, consultants and management team in moving to the cloud."

Linda Rose, CPA, President/CEO, Rose Business Solutions Inc.

"The growth of customers asking about the Cloud is accelerating. Microsoft's commitment to the Cloud is providing credibility. Our experience in supporting an eco-system of over 700 Microsoft partners offering Cloud services is that their success is directly linked to the quality of their planning. This book will be a huge help in removing the 'where do I start' challenge as partners consider adding Cloud ERP to their portfolio."

Doug Tutus, CEO, NewLease

Author

Stephen Parker

Head of Cloud Strategy, NewLease Pty Ltd

A business executive and Cloud Computing specialist, with over 20 years experience of taking technology investment decisions and delivering solutions on the leading edge of IT in Enterprise and SMB companies.

With the lessons learnt from the transformation and trade sale of an established but struggling SMB on-premises ERP business to a cloud eProcurement business and over 12 years of delivering web based business solutions, Stephen is now focused on helping businesses maximize their commercial opportunities in the emerging Cloud market.

Stephen is a member of Microsoft's corporate Cloud Services Partner Advisory Council, provides associate services to industry analysts and has written a variety of books covering the Cloud space.

Acknowledgements

Books tell stories that bring together ideas from multiple sources and with many contributors. This book is no different and so my thanks go out to those who have helped, in large part or small and whether consciously or not.

In particular the support of David Ford, Senior Director, Gartner, Kim Smith, Director, Microsoft Business Solutions Cloud Partner Strategy and Jeff Edwards, Director, Microsoft Business Solutions ERP Partner Strategy has been invaluable and I would like to say a special thanks to them.

Contributors

David Ford

David Ford focuses on business strategy and innovation with Gartner Consulting. He has over 10 years of experience working on a variety of internal and external business, marketing and communication strategies in industries ranging from technology providers to the public sector. Recently, David has been thinking a lot about the Cloud.

David holds a Bachelor of Arts degree in English Literature from the University of California Santa Barbara, a Master of Arts in English Literature (Shakespeare) from New York University, and a Master of Business Administration from the Peter Drucker School of Management, Claremont Graduate University

Kim Smith

Kim Smith serves as the Director of Worldwide Partner Strategy for Microsoft Business Solutions Cloud and Customer Relationship Management (CRM) products and offerings at Microsoft Corporation driving partnership and channel development globally. Kim has been at Microsoft for over ten years leading in roles such as driving the international partner strategy for Worldwide Public Sector, business strategy and development for the Microsoft Business Division, and global business operations and partner strategy for the Microsoft Services Division.

With over 24 years of experience managing the successful implementation of global business solutions and enterprise technology initiatives across Fortune 1000 companies and public sector organizations, Kim has led business development and venture integration efforts required to transition organizations from service, software, and hardware providers to business solution delivery leaders. She is a published speaker and patented process innovator with published industry and technology white papers and has maintained leadership positions in technology and business councils worldwide.

Foreword

The business applications market is evolving rapidly to meet the ever changing needs of customers, from small businesses balancing their budgets to large enterprises with a need for specialized applications working in unison with complex, centralized business processes. There is tremendous opportunity to take advantage of new technologies and create processes which are more standard, decentralized, and cloud enabled to better serve suppliers, buyers, and consumers of goods and services. Innovation in cloud computing will continue to drive rapid evolution of technology exponentially over the next few years; it will be a journey where we should expect to see an increasing amount of consumerized influence over the experiences.

As users across small, medium and large enterprises take increasing advantage of cloud based systems, their expectations and demand will match what they experience as consumers in their life outside of work. They'll expect that systems constantly predict and adapt to their behavior and usage, similar to what we know from search engines today. It's the individual's behavior in combination with that of users in their broader organization, industry and segment that defines the user's expectations, and it will be increasingly hard to meet such requirements without the use of cloud.

It will be critical for companies to align use of on-premises and cloud components in their quest to be dynamic businesses, constantly enabling them to adapt to market forces, business demand, economic and geopolitical constraints and not the least; new business opportunities.

The use of dynamic technology delivered through on-premises software and/or cloud-based services will take an increasingly important place as companies build, drive and influence the sentiment around their brand, and I believe that we, as business leaders in the IT industry, need to understand how to deliver software, services and experiences that enables that. We need to take calculated risks with cloud orientation in our business models so we can constantly advance ability to deliver new levels of value to our customers and change the market.

Join me now to learn how ERP in the Cloud will fundamentally change the future of how we do business.

Christian Pedersen,

General Manager, Dynamics ERP Cloud and AX Product Management, Microsoft Business Solutions, Microsoft Corporation

Table of Contents

1 The Clouds are everywhere 1

2 ERP in the Cloud? 7

3 Ask the Smart Questions 13

4 A Time for Planning 15

5 Questions for my business 17

6 Questions about my customer 35

7 Questions for vendors 51

8 Call to Action 65

Who should read this book?

People like you and me

People like you and me. This book is not technical, nor was it ever intended to be. It is aimed squarely at those who see IT as a utility that should be consumed to serve the business. Not the reverse. People like you and me. This book is intended to be a catalyst for action aimed at a range of people inside and outside your organization. Here are just a few, and why it is relevant to them.

Thought leaders in existing Microsoft Dynamics partners

The primary audience for this book is the thought leaders within businesses that have already made a commitment to Microsoft and specifically the Microsoft Dynamics product offerings. The significant investment by Microsoft into Cloud enabling their range of software assets and specifically the Microsoft Dynamics products has the potential to significantly disrupt the Line of Business market. Your existing skills are likely to provide you with core assets for this new Cloud future. However any disruptive change creates the opportunity for new entrants into a market and now is the time to start planning so you are not caught napping and your assets continue to be strengths to the business rather than milestones around your neck.

This book will provide key insights and the smart questions that will help with this planning process.

Owner/Leaders of Microsoft Partner businesses

The Cloud has the potential to change the deployment and cost models for provisioning line of business applications. Does this open an opportunity for you to enhance your existing service provision by including cloud enabled versions of Microsoft Dynamics products? Many traditional service providers are already adding Office365 and CRM Online to their service catalog and driving revenue grow. Does ERP offer another revenue opportunity? This book will provide ideas that may start a consideration of these wider opportunities.

Strategy planners with IT and Telco service providers

The carrot of services that will drive both new direct revenue streams and also support/enhance existing revenue e.g. "on-net" has been dangling in front of IT and Telco service providers for some time. Yet success in this area has been inconsistent for many reasons. One of the major ones has been the early adopter status of the Cloud provisioning of core LoB applications. The growing success and maturing of the market is increasingly shifting this status to early majority and thus opening real opportunities. However there are new business and consulting skills required for successful deployment of these services.

This book will help you to understand the factors that traditional ERP providers are considering and hence areas that you will need to address and/or create to take advantage of differentiated and disruptive thinking.

Line of Business Application Owners

Although this book is aimed primarily at "service provider" organizations, as the owner of Line of Business applications within your company you may find value in understanding the direction your service providers and their underlying vendors are working towards. As always insight is one of the starting points for planning.

How to use this book

This book is intended to be the catalyst for action. We hope that the ideas and examples inspire you to act. So, do whatever you need to do to make this book useful. Use Post-it notes, write on it, rip it apart, or read it quickly in one sitting. Whatever works for you. We hope this becomes your most dog-eared book.

Chapter 1

The Clouds are everywhere

I am not afraid of tomorrow, for I have seen yesterday and I love today.

William Allen White (American Journalist, 1868 – 1944)

Cloud, Cloud, Cloud

IT does not matter where you look or listen there is a "cloud" message aimed at your customers and it is coming from all directions. This is not just about messaging to IT types, this is directed at everyone.

Vendors are pushing their marketing departments to ensure their Cloud message is being heard, even if this is simply a case of loud shouting without a clear and coherent story behind it (as long as people know we are in the game we can sort out how we are playing later!!). Journalists covering all areas of business and consumer land are writing articles. Some are providing informed debate about the Cloud, both the benefits and the real concerns that need to be addressed. Others are simply jumping on the Cloud bandwagon and enjoying the cheap journalism that this allows.

And this cycle is a self-reinforcing one. The more the vendors shout, the more the journalists write and the more people start asking about the cloud. Seeing this customer interest encourages more vendors and journalists to join in and around we go.

What is Cloud Computing?

There is of course the cynical answer that the cloud is anything the customer wants it to be. After all it is simply a phrase that has no more meaning than Desktop Computing. This has some merit, on the basis that it is, after all, our customers that should be driving our behavior and if Cloud Computing is a concept they can rally around then so be it.

However as service providers and trusted advisors we need to be able to make sense of this concept and provide guidance. To that end there are a number of definitions that are starting to gain traction with the one from the National Institute of Standards & Technology, US Dept. of Commerce rising to the top[1]. To paraphrase, there are certain essential characteristics that need to be present for a service to call itself a Cloud service:

- On-demand self-service (DIY)
- Broad network access (anywhere, any tool access)
- Resource pooling (multi-tenant, shared resources)
- Rapid elasticity (Scale up/down as needed)
- Measured service (transparency of utilisation)

There are also the following services models:

- Software as a Service (SaaS)
- Platform as a Service (PaaS)
- Infrastructure as a Service (IaaS)

And finally these deployment models:

- Private Cloud
- Community Cloud
- Public Cloud
- Hybrid Cloud

Naturally, even as this definition is beginning to gain traction there is already a blurring of the lines between the service models. Add

---

[1] *http://www.nist.gov/itl/cloud/index.cfm*

to this the IT industries propensity for integrating new ideas into the existing ones rather than replacing them, then it is likely that the Hybrid deployment model will be the dominant one going forward.

Growing Success

Not all of this noise is translating into understanding and action, however it is creating a growing awareness. At this point it would be easy to close your eyes and ears and wait, hoping that the noise goes away. While this may be tempting it would be ignoring the fact that behind the noise there is a real message of growing success and a disruptive change that is sweeping the IT and business landscape.

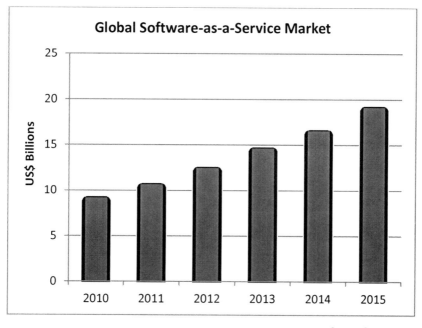

Source: Gartner 2011

There are massive investments from existing vendors and the disruptive nature of the Cloud is providing opportunities for new entrants, both small niche players and future global brands.

Microsoft Global Investments in Online Services

Data centers:

- Global Foundation Services (the Microsoft data center delivery vehicle) have 6 publically announced data centers that cost hundreds of thousands of USD each

R&D:

- 90% of R&D focused on Cloud efforts in 2011[2]

Microsoft Online Products in market:

- Microsoft Office 365

- Microsoft Dynamics CRM Online

- Windows InTune

Subscription software revenue streams are growing across all workloads. The changing nature of how revenue is recorded in a subscription world also means that these figures are a genuine reflection of growth as they represent actually usage.

This is different to the on-premises measures that can be distorted. Whether by a channel packed with unwanted inventory, or customers who have "enterprise agreements" and are recorded as having 3 products, but only really use 2.

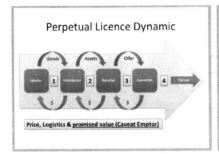
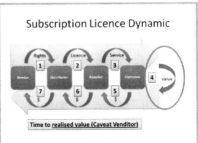

The high growth of Microsoft's Service Provider License Agreement (SPLA) program is another example of this:

---

[2] http://www.microsoft.com/presspass/exec/steve/2010/03-04Cloud.mspx

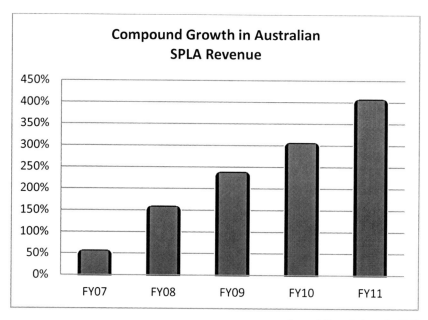

Compound Growth in Australian SPLA Revenue

Source: Microsoft Australia 2010

Most crucially the drivers for this increasing interest in the Cloud are coming from your customers rather than being a marketing tool for the IT industry to push new versions of existing products

CIO technologies	Ranking of technologies CIOs selected as one of their top 3 priorities in 2011			
Ranking	*2011*	*2010*	*2009*	*2008*
Cloud computing	1	2	16	*
Virtualization	2	1	3	3
Mobile technologies	3	6	12	12
IT management	4	10	*	*
Business intelligence (BI)	5	5	1	1
Networking, voice and data communications	6	4	6	7
Enterprise applications	7	11	2	2
Collaboration technologies	8	10	5	8
Infrastructure	9	14	7	6
Web 2.0	10	3	15	15

*New response category

Source: Gartner 2011 CIO Agenda – Top Priorities

There is also increasing research that indicates that SaaS applications are no longer seen as "new" technology. For example Gartner research[3] identifies that 28% of businesses in the Enterprise Application market have been using SaaS for 5+ years. Importantly this reaches a tipping point level of 46% if you consider 3+ years' experience.

So the Cloud in general is gaining traction, but what about Line of Business Solutions; is the Cloud ready for them?

---

[3] Gartner Software as a Service, Enterprise Application Markets, Worldwide, 2010 – N=172

Chapter

2

ERP in the Cloud?

For the majority of us, the past is a regret, the future an experiment.

Mark Twain (Humorist & Writer, 1835 - 1910)

Are we Ready?

DESPITE the hype and noise there would appear to be some real credibility around the delivery of Cloud services. But are we really ready to trust the Cloud with our Line of Business applications?

Outsourcing the provision of email to a Cloud or Hosting provider may be a simple step. Although a key part of business, email has reached a commodity status and the use of the internet is already central to its working.

Core Line of Business applications on the other hand are seen by many as needing a different approach and maybe for good reason:

- The data they process sits at the heart of the business
- Real time access is central to their use
- Critical business decisions rely on their accuracy and availability
- Refresh cycles are typically 5 years or greater

With all of this in mind the received wisdom is that Line of Business Applications and ERP in particular is a more conservative market and will be later to ride the Cloud wave.

Where CRM leads others follow

Despite this thought process there is evidence to the contrary, showing that the market (your customers) are being far more creative than anticipated and driving far greater use of the Cloud for core business services than predicted.

 Who would have thought that CRM would be one of the "poster children" for the Cloud revolution? This is after all where our key business secrets, our relationships, the stories and insights we have about our customers and competitors are managed. If anything this information is even more sensitive than accounting data and yet we have seen the rise of Salesforce as a pure play SaaS provider with revenues of USD1Bn+.

Businesses of all sizes are using online services such as eBay, Amazon and PayPal. These not only provision the online shopping experience, but also offer billing services, cash collection, order delivery notification and other capabilities that could be considered part of ERP.

There are a number of established small business Accounting software packages that are being offered as a "hosted" service[4] and startups who are delivering pure play Cloud ERP solutions[5].

What next for ERP?

Despite ongoing acquisitions within the ERP industry it is still a fragmented market and the emergence of new Cloud ERP startups has simply added to this fragmentation. For the mass market adoption of Cloud ERP to take place it will require one of the industry leaders to make a real commitment to the Cloud. This will not just be a marketing launch or an offering that stays in private

---

[4] Quicken via Reckon Online in Australia *http://online.reckon.com.au/*
[5] *http://www.xero.com/*

beta for multiple years. It will have to be an "all-in" moment that is not a side experiment but central to the forward strategy of the business.

Furthermore ERP, more than many areas relies on the support of 3rd parties – accountants, technical experts, business change experts etc. Cloud success will therefore require more than just the vendor commitment to the cloud technology and the delivery of a robust delivery platform, but also a strong ecosystem that is both supportive of and supported by the vendor.

The Cloud shift is a disruptive one and will lead to:

- Different assumptions about the capability required (think MP3 i.e. less quality for increased convenience)
- Opportunities to address business areas previously outside traditional ERP (size, geography), or provide access to previously excluded staff (mobility, remote offices)
- The arrival of new providers (Telcos, SI's, ISV's adding ERP capability, etc.)

The question will be how you handle this disruptive opportunity? Will this be a revolutionary leap for your business where you use this as a chance to fundamentally shift your business? Will there be a new business off-shoot where you focus your cloud efforts? Or will this be integrated into your existing model? Experience from other research such as "Building a Successful Microsoft Business Productivity Online Services Practice"[6] suggests that the key to success will be around Commitment and Creativity rather than the business model itself.

Find your path - Hybrid Cloud

A key factor to consider as part of your "creativity" will be reviewing your notions of *where* ERP solutions are deployed. The term *Hybrid Cloud* is already being used to describe the models where the workloads are spread across on-premises, partner hosted (private cloud) and public cloud. Even with the significant Cloud commitments from ERP vendors it is likely that certain workloads will be better suited to public cloud deployments.

---

[6] *https://partner.microsoft.com/global/40152835*

Understanding the capabilities of the public cloud services and using your knowledge and creativity to match these to your customer needs will be a key part of your success. And for your customers you will provide them with the options for an evolutionary journey rather a revolutionary leap.

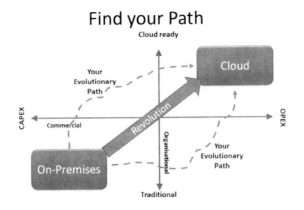

Challenges to Consider

In mature markets, customer needs and supplier offers connect over time through a sort of marketplace osmosis. However in emerging and disruptive markets this same assumption cannot be made. Customers may have defined new needs and associated different benefits, which can lead to the existing value proposition of the supplier offer becoming disconnected.

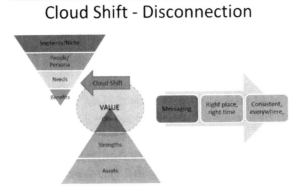

In this scenario where the "generic industry understanding" of the value proposition has shifted, it will be key to ensure that rather than being "Interesting to many" offers will need to be "Essential to few". Unless the offer is sufficiently precise and targets the "essential" needs of the customer then there is the risk of initial excitement falling into the "too difficult bucket". The promised benefits will founder as the "How?" blockers come into play.

When defining the "essential" offer it is likely that there will be recognition that not all business opportunities are born equal. It may be necessary to consider the use of filters that can help avoid selling to businesses that are just not ready for the Cloud.

- Those with solid legal or compliance reasons that will raise challenges around data location, security etc.
- Concerns raised by your customer about their customers Cloud concerns
- Emotional concerns about the Cloud

Please note that in most cases these issues can be addressed, however just because you are intellectually capable of convincing a customer to overcome their concerns does not mean they should be in your initial 10% of sales targets!!

As mentioned before the shift to a subscription revenue model changes the dynamic from Caveat Emptor (Buyer Beware) to Caveat Venditor (Seller beware). The customer will expect to get quick "time to value" and if they do not, they will consider leaving. They are not tied into the high levels of upfront investment that encourage them to spend more to make it work. In the 2011 Panorama ERP Report[7], 21% of SMB respondents reported realizing less that 30% of the projected benefits, with a further 27% realized less that 50%. These "sins of the past" will be unacceptable in the "delivered value" world of the Cloud. However more positively this creates the opportunity for the "ready to go" nature of Cloud services to address these concerns and drive quick adoption and high customer satisfaction.

Skills Evolution

By definition a hosted or Cloud service will be pre-installed on an underlying infrastructure. This will therefore have an impact on the amount of "engineering" resources required, with a shift to more consultative style services. If you are an engineering business

---

[7] http://panorama-consulting.com/resource-center/2011-erp-report/

by nature who does consulting as a necessary evil, then you may have to consider how your skills will evolve.

Skills Evolution

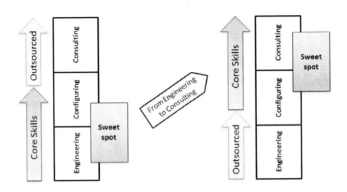

Despite the more conservative positioning of ERP in the market it appears as if we are approaching a tipping point. However there also seem to be challenges that I will need to address. Should I embrace or avoid? What next for my business?

Chapter

Ask the Smart Questions

If I have seen further it is by standing on the shoulders of giants

Isaac Newton (Scientist, 1643 – 1727)

S MART Questions is about giving you valuable insights or "the Smarts". Normally these are only gained through years of painful and costly experience. Whether you already have a general understanding of the subject and need to take it to the next level or are starting from scratch, you need to make sure you ask the Smart Questions. We aim to short circuit that learning process, by providing the expertise of the 'giants' that Isaac Newton referred to.

Not all the questions will necessarily be new or staggeringly insightful. The value you get from the information will clearly vary. It depends on your job role and previous experience. We call this the 3Rs.

The 3 Rs

Some of the questions will be in areas where you know all the answers so they will be **Reinforced** in your mind.

You may have forgotten certain areas so the book will **Remind** you.

And other questions may be things you have never considered and will be **Revealed** to you.

How do you use Smart Questions?

The structure of the questions is set out in Chapter 4, and the questions are in Chapters 5 through 7. The questions are laid out in a series of structured and ordered tables with the questions in one column and the explanation of why it matters alongside. We have also provided a checkbox so that you can mark which questions are relevant to your particular situation.

A quick scan down the first column in the list of questions should give you a general feel of where you are for each question vs. the 3Rs. At the highest level they are a sanity check or checklist of areas to consider. Just one question may save you a whole heap of cash or heartache.

We trust that you will find real insights. There may be some "aha" moments. Hopefully not too many sickening, "head in the hands – what were we thinking" moments. The questions could be used in your internal planning meetings to inform or at least prompt the debate. Alternatively they could shape the discussion you have with Microsoft about their ERP in the Cloud plans.

Probably the most critical role of the questions is that they reveal risks that you had not considered. On the flip side they may also open up your thinking to opportunities that you had not considered. Balancing the opportunities and the risks, and then agreeing what is realistically achievable is the key to formulating strategy.

And finally

Please remember that these questions are NOT intended to be a prescriptive list that must be followed slavishly from beginning to end. It is also inevitable that the list of questions is not exhaustive and we are confident that with the help of the community the list of Smart Questions will grow.

We also understand that not all of the questions will apply to all businesses. However we encourage you to read them all as there may be a nugget of truth that can be adapted to your circumstances.

Above all we do hope that it provides a guide or a pointer to the areas that may be valuable to you and helps with the "3 Rs".

A Time for Planning

In preparing for battle I have always found that plans are useless, but planning is indispensible.

Dwight D Eisenhower (US General, 1890 – 1969)

A S Eisenhower suggests, it is often the act of planning itself that leads to success rather than the plan that the process produces. Thinking about the why, what, where, when, and how type questions as part of a planning process will assist in clarifying the strategy that is right for you and your customers. This may lead to the conclusion that ERP and the Cloud are not right for you at the moment. In which case you can formulate and communicate a clear and positive strategy that supports this.

However if you conclude that ERP in the Cloud is the way forward then you can make a confident commitment and use your creative talents to arrive into the market in a timely and prepared manner.

The Smart Questions to support your thinking have been structured across the following 3 chapters as outlined below

Chapter 5: Questions for my business

1. **Section 1** – Motivation
2. **Section 2** – State of my organization
3. **Section 3** – Commercial considerations

Chapter 6: Questions about my customer

1. **Section 1** – What is their cloud motivation
2. **Section 2** – Questions about their business
3. **Section 3** – Technology

Chapter 7: Questions for vendors

1. **Section 1** – Capability
2. **Section 2** –Credibility
3. **Section 3** – Commitment

Chapter 5

Questions for my business

When it comes to the future, there are three kinds of people: those who let it happen, those who make it happen, and those who wonder what happened.

John M. Richardson, Jr. (American Academic, 1938 -)

I N order to make decisions that will enable your organisation to achieve its goals you need to start by looking inwards. You need to make informed decisions about how and where you invest your time and energy to get to where you want to be.

It is important that we remember that Cloud Computing is simply

an umbrella marketing term to describe how software can be provided to your customers. Cloud Computing is not an end in itself. Its only purpose is to assist in meeting business goals or addressing challenges or issues. Therefore it is critical that you are clear about what is driving you to consider delivering ERP solutions through the Cloud. Being clear about this will inform the questions for your organization and help set a successful strategy.

If your business message is not clear to you, how can you expect to be able to articulate it to your customers, your partners and Microsoft?

5.1 Motivation

This section is all about understanding what is motivating you to consider an ERP Cloud solution. After all it is too easy to get caught up in hype of the latest 'new idea'.

Will Cloud Computing enable you to capture or defend a market? Is it being demanded of you by customers? Can you reduce sales cycles by side stepping barriers put up by the customer's IT department?

Be clear about these drivers or goals as they will inform your other questions.

☒	Question	Why this matters
☐	5.1.1 Is Cloud ERP an evolution or a revolution?	In the early stages of Cloud, it is sometimes hard to separate reality from vendor and media hype. While almost everybody believes in a SaaS future, common wisdom from tech pundits is ERP will be the last enterprise application to move into the cloud. The reality is Cloud ERP solutions are emerging and, as the market matures, new use cases are surfacing (think an SMB using eBay / PayPal to facilitate order to cash). The combination of these dynamics suggests that while over the next few years Cloud ERP is likely to be an evolution, there is a looming inflection point where maturing vendor solutions and emerging customer use cases suggest a revolution
☐	5.1.2 Is Cloud ERP a parallel offering?	Cloud facilitates two-tier ERP where applications supporting complex centralized business processes remain on-premises and standard decentralized business processes are SaaS enabled. The trick for vendors aligning on-premises and Cloud components of an ERP solution with customer need is creating an optimal solution, and avoiding cannibalization.
☐	5.1.3 Have you lost business because you did not have a Cloud ERP offering?	Losing business tends to be a compelling reason to consider alternative approaches. Given that Cloud ERP is likely to be more evolution than revolution over the next few years, vendors are unlikely to have experienced significant negative impact to revenue. There are many reasons why the time may not be right to actively position Cloud ERP as a viable solution for your customers (business process complexity, security, data location). Having said that, Cloud ERP is less if than when and now is the time to begin thinking about the impact on your customers and your business

☒	Question	Why this matters
☐	5.1.4 Is there pressure from your customers to explore Cloud ERP solutions?	Even if you have not lost business directly, a sign that Cloud ERP is on the way is the extent to which your customers are talking and asking. Even if you know that Cloud ERP is not right for your customers today, you should start talking to them about it with them to anticipate future needs
☐	5.1.5 Would your reputation for being a market innovator suffer without a Cloud ERP solution?	You may have built your reputation based on always being on the leading edge. Cloud ERP creates marketing and positioning opportunities (leading vendors like Microsoft and IBM are not spending a lot of time promoting traditional on-premises solutions). However, as with any emerging market, you may need to be careful which vendors you decide to partner with on Cloud ERP
☐	5.1.6 Are you perceived as conservative and want to add a little edge to your offering?	While marketing tends to focus on the latest greatest thing, the reality is most businesses are run on last year's technology. Most companies are conservative by nature and unlikely to take a flier on an emerging technology from a new vendor. Your business depends on maintaining safe trusted advisor relationships with your customers. Adding Cloud ERP may add an edge to your business, but this needs to be balanced against your customers' needs for safe solutions. The reality is, over the next couple years, Cloud ERP will be additive to your traditional business. The fact is, it is a bonus

☒	**Question**	**Why this matters**
☐	5.1.7 Are you increasingly required to sell to both business and IT customers?	As technology matures, it tends to become 'friendlier' to business users. This trend is likely to accelerate with Cloud ERP, which means you will be increasingly selling to both IT and the business. Your ability to effectively interact with business users, to speak their language, will be a critical differentiator as Cloud ERP emerges and matures
☐	5.1.8 Are you having problems acquiring new customers because you did not have a Cloud ERP offering?	While customers may decide to keep their ERP solution on-premises, they increasingly expect to be given a Cloud option. At a minimum, you need to be ready to explain what Cloud ERP potentially means and how your customers can potentially enjoy the benefits so, even if they stay on-premises, they can make an informed decision
☐	5.1.9 Are your existing competitors offering a Cloud ERP solution?	Just as you are now thinking about the Cloud, it is likely that your competitors are as well and you need to be positioned to respond with a compelling story that explains what Cloud ERP means for your customers and how you can help
☐	5.1.10 Are new ISVs / VARs entering your market with a Cloud ERP offering?	One of the reasons for considering Cloud ERP is it creates opportunities to extend geographically and/or monetize vertical business process expertise. Unfortunately, just as this is good for you, it also creates opportunities for ISVs / VARs to extend into your market. One of the challenges here is that you may not even be aware that these businesses exist to saying nothing of the new reality that they are competitors

☒ Question	Why this matters
☐ 5.1.11 Are your partners providing Cloud ERP offerings?	While Cloud ERP represents a transition of IT responsibility from end users to vendors, it still requires an ecosystem to sell and deliver. To the extent your current partners do not offer and have no plans to offer a Cloud ERP solution, then your business runs the risk of increasing irrelevance as Cloud ERP matures
☐ 5.1.12 Are industry analysts for your sector predicting an inflection point in the Cloud ERP market?	Arguably the safe time to start moving on Cloud ERP is when the analysts in your sector are predicting an inflection point. While you may miss the opportunity to be on the bleeding edge, you will benefit from being able to make an informed decision about partners and solutions. As always, there is a fine balance between getting too far in front of the market versus being behind. Having said that, Cloud ERP is emerging as a hot topic with industry analysts, suggesting that now is the time to think about your balance point between early adopter versus fast follower
☐ 5.1.13 Is the media talking about Cloud ERP?	It is hard to find media coverage of ERP that does not reference the Cloud in some form. While the ability of Cloud ERP to provide real value to customers ultimately determines the adoption curve, the current media hype creates a strong signal that Cloud ERP is real

☒	Question	Why this matters
☐	5.1.14 Can you increase the barriers to entry for potential competitors?	Being seen as providing a Cloud ERP offering may in itself enhance the market's perception of you. It may be part of your business model to be seen as leading edge. It also may send a clear signal to your competitors that you intend to lead in the Cloud. Any change is an opportunity to increase barriers to entry for potential competitors. Given the reality that Cloud ERP may look attractive to new competitors, offering a Cloud ERP solution may dissuade new competitors from entering your market.
☐	5.1.15 Could you gain first mover advantages by adopting a Cloud ERP solution?	A first mover advantage has the potential to make your competitors' strengths irrelevant by providing customers with something so different that you change the game. For example, Xbox Kinect set a world record as the fastest growing consumer technology in history. It did this by fundamentally changing the way people interacted with technology and creating games that were meant to be played by groups of people sharing the experience together in the same physical space. This opened the market from hard core gamers to a range of new customers who enjoy playing together with friends and family
☐	5.1.16 Will Cloud ERP give you a competitive advantage?	Being seen as offering a Cloud ERP solution may in itself enhance the market's perception of you. It may be important to your business and customers to be seen as leading edge. Change creates opportunities for sustainable competitive advantage and Cloud ERP represents a transformation in the way solutions are delivered

5.2 State of my organization

You are happy that your motivations for incorporating Cloud based ERP offerings into your business strategy are sound and you are now fired up, enthusiastic and ready to get started.

But before we dive in let us start by looking if there are banana skins that we could slip on? What road blocks are there that could stop us in our tracks?

☒ Question	Why this matters
5.2.1 Is your business under pressure from the economic crisis and in need of a breakout strategy?	The recent economic crisis put tremendous pressure on service providers and, some, did not survive. If you had to lay off staff or downsize the business to survive over the past few years, then you know how hard it is to weather market crises. However, provided your organization and investors are clear about the risks and costs associated with changing your business model, now may be a good time for reinvention. The key is not to throw out the aspects of your business that resonate with customers. There are customers who need your traditional offerings and, in order to survive and thrive in the future, you need a sound business plan that considers how the market is likely to evolve and your role in it. The combination of turbulent markets and accelerating Cloud transformation creates headlines about businesses that claim to be Cloud based with no current revenue and multi-million dollar valuations – remember these are NOT the norm
5.2.2 Is the owner/board supportive of a Cloud ERP strategy?	Without the support of the owners/board all the enthusiasm in the world will not drive a Cloud ERP strategy forward. This is an obvious but key area that needs to be clarified.
5.2.3 Does your organization's culture embrace change?	Not all businesses are naturally comfortable with change. In fact, most are not. This is probably a good thing otherwise we could quickly end up in chaos! However, if your company culture is conservative, then you will need to be prepared to provide greater evidence of the value Cloud ERP can bring and insure that key internal players and stakeholders in your organization are supportive

☒	Question	Why this matters
☐	5.2.4 How does Cloud ERP fit into your existing business Goal?	If your current goals are already consistent with a Cloud approach to delivering services then this is remove many challenges. On the other hand if the Cloud will require you to revisit your business goals then you will need to factor the time required for this in your plans
☐	5.2.5 Will your Cloud plans fit within existing budget plans?	Existing funds that can support your Cloud plans will clearly accelerate things. Otherwise you will either have to factor in the budget cycle delays, try and wrestle funds from other areas or look for new funding.
☐	5.2.6 Can you invest in sales and marketing for a Cloud ERP solution?	Traditional IT services tends to focus on selling discrete projects where success is measured by utilization of delivery resources. Cloud ERP shifts this model to selling continuous services where success is measured by the volume of customers. Consequently, Cloud ERP typically emphasizes sales and marketing versus delivery resources. It also means a new set of marketing skills required to generate volume and sales resources that can sell to both the business and IT
☐	5.2.7 Can you address new markets?	With the reach of the internet and new Cloud ERP opportunities like application marketplaces, can you offer your solutions to geographies outside your home base? This is a compelling opportunity that Cloud ERP facilitates. However, although many of the traditional barriers to entry may be reduced, you may still need to consider partnering with companies to provide local sales support and training or on-site consulting where required

☒	Question	Why this matters
☐	5.2.8 Can you address new industry verticals?	As Cloud ERP emerges and matures, your ability to speak to the specific industry needs of your customers becomes critically important. For customers, vertical expertise is what allows you to position as a trusted advisor, providing a sense of comfort that helps them realistically assess the risk and the benefits associated with adopting Cloud solutions. For your business, vertical expertise creates opportunities for you to build vertical specific applications that can be resold in application marketplaces on a global basis. For Cloud ERP vendor partners, your vertical expertise creates opportunities to build custom solutions for industry niches. The value of industry vertical expertise to Cloud ERP cannot be understated, which means that this is less a question than an imperative for your business
☐	5.2.9 Can you market and sell to business customers?	One of the promises of the Cloud is a dramatic simplification of the way IT is delivered. In a world where applications can literally be turned on and off with minimal up-front investment, business users can trial applications – frequently without the knowledge of the IT shop. Indeed, business users have been one of the primary drivers of Cloud CRM adoption. The ability to sell to business customers based on a deep understanding of their business has always been important, but it becomes critical with Cloud ERP

☒	Question	Why this matters
☐	5.2.10 Do you have application development competencies in your organization?	The application marketplaces offered by leading Cloud vendors create opportunities for you to develop and sell vertical applications outside of your focus markets. However, to the extent your organization fits the VAR model, you may not have the internal resources required to convert your industry vertical expertise to software
☐	5.2.11 What percentage of your workforce is devoted to development and integration?	It is likely that a core competency of your organization has been development, integration, and customization required to enable traditional ERP solutions. With Cloud ERP, these services will evolve towards configuration, training, consulting, business process change, and hybrid solution integration. Customers will continue to need service providers, but they will be increasingly looking for vendors who understand their business and can help them profitably grow versus a deep understanding of their IT shop

5.3 Commercial considerations

Cloud Computing opens up a number of new business models; i.e. how you get paid. Not all of them will be appropriate; however any change of business model can have profound implications on the organization, motivation and compensation of both the front and back office operations.

The move to Cloud Computing also has implications on the metrics you use to judge the health and wellbeing of the company and the way you manage the finances.

In many ways the models for commercialization of the Cloud have been framed in a way that is friendly to start ups and potentially challenging or even threatening to established companies. Does this mean that all established businesses must throw everything away and reinvent themselves? Or can they look at the new options and consider how these can be best utilized within their existing business? For some there will be a revolution and for others an evolutionary approach will be the right way. The real point is that there are choices.

This section cannot cover the whole subject area of commercial considerations. However, we trust that even where we have missed something that is relevant to you, the process of reviewing these questions will help you generate your own areas to consider.

☒ **Question**	**Why this matters**
☐ 5.3.1 Is your customer base stale?	Service providers tend to rely on selling discrete projects to the same customer as they work through various technology refresh cycles. Conversely, success with Cloud ERP depends on be able to attract new customers. To the extent that your success is critically reliant on selling to the same customer base, you will need to consider the kinds of sales and marketing investments and competencies you will need to develop to drive the significant volume of new customers required to make Cloud ERP profitable
☐ 5.3.2 What percentage of revenue do you devote to marketing?	Many service providers rely on long-term relationships to market their services and devote a relatively small percentage of revenue to marketing. The total investment in marketing will need to change in order for Cloud ERP to be successful. A key consideration for your business as you adopt Cloud ERP is where is this marketing investment going to come from? To the extent that you do not have the resources to increase marketing spend, then you should look at Cloud ERP vendors who are willing to invest in marketing on your behalf

☒ Question	Why this matters
☐ 5.3.3 Will Cloud ERP make it easier for customers to purchase your offering?	Conceptually, one of the promises of cloud is flexible payments terms with minimal upfront investment. The reality is the way a customer pays for Cloud ERP varies vendor to vendor. To the extent that you can provide flexible payment terms, for example, monthly billing rather than a large upfront fee, then the budget holder may have authority to sign off on the costs directly. Also being able to OpEx the costs with a clear option to cease payment without penalty may reduce the concerns about lock in and budget constraints. However, remember that for some businesses CapEx is still their preferred budgeting approach, so make sure you can help them 'capitalize' their investment
☐ 5.3.4 Can you reduce time to market?	Cloud ERP provides the opportunity to introduce new ideas and functionality to customers at a much faster rate than traditional on-premises models. This creates opportunities to dramatically shorten time to market for your services
☐ 5.3.5 Can you shorten your sales cycle with a Cloud ERP offering?	By removing the need to customize and install ERP and being able to trial the user experience directly to the business user with minimal IT involvement, Cloud ERP promises to shorten the sales cycle while helping accelerate time to value for your customers

☒	Question	Why this matters
☐	5.3.6 Can your sales force adapt to longer term incentives?	The annuity pricing used for many Cloud offerings brings the issues of sales commission and rewards sharply into focus. Sales staff who are used to big sales bonuses associated with selling discrete 'deals' may find it difficult to work with longer term incentive models. However, given the relationship between incentives and the current economic crisis, one could argue there is a general cultural shift towards longer term reward models that will hopefully align incentives with long term business success
☐	5.3.7 How many of your internal resources are devoted to traditional ERP development and integration?	As Cloud ERP emerges, traditional development and integration services will evolve towards configuration, training, consulting, business process change, and hybrid solution integration. This means the internal resources you have devoted to traditional development and integration will need to learn new skills to stay relevant to your business. This will be an evolution not a revolution, but creating a clear plan for how organizational competencies will need to shift, the timeframe, and what this means to your workforce is critical to a successful transition to the Cloud
☐	5.3.8 Do you generate significant revenue from traditional ERP support?	Cloud ERP does not fundamentally change the support model. In fact, it may create new sales opportunities that will come from support as customers call you to talk through trials and the updates and changes in application functionality that are likely to be accelerated in the Cloud. In fact, your support team may become a primary contact point with customers. Realizing these opportunities may require new help desk skills and training such as sales skills

☒	Question	Why this matters
☐	5.3.9 Do you have the financial resources to fund the transition to an annuity based services model?	Switching from a model that is reliant on software licenses and discrete services to an annuity model may have long term benefits in terms of predictability and valuation, however in the short term it can create a significant cash flow issue. If availability of capital is likely to be an issue for you as you move to Cloud ERP, then you need to talk with your CFO, accountants, and investors to make sure you have the cash to fund the transition. You should also consider partnering with a Cloud ERP vendor who is committed to your long term success and can provide support such as financing where you get paid upfront for part or all of the contract value or favorable partnership terms where your business gets a material percentage of the annuity revenue
☐	5.3.10 Will there be a loss of revenue during the transition?	As Cloud ERP matures, customers are going to be wary about investing in traditional on-premises solutions. At the same time, Cloud ERP is maturing and customers may not understand that current solutions will be unable to meet their full needs. What this means is customers will be looking to you for advice on how to handle the transition to Cloud ERP. So while there may be an incremental loss in revenue, your ability to play the role of trusted advisor with your customers is critical to long term success

☒ Question	Why this matters
☐ 5.3.11 How likely is Cloud ERP to cannibalize your traditional business?	Over the near term, the reality is Cloud ERP will not eat into your traditional business. However, as Cloud ERP solutions mature and gain wider market acceptance, they will be an increasingly larger share of your business. Market transformations generally have inflection points as early adopters give way to the early majority so one of the dynamics you need to be prepared for is you may experience limited pressure from Cloud ERP on your current business and then, suddenly, experience a significant erosion as the market takes off
☐ 5.3.12 Do you have an exit strategy?	It is not unusual for businesses to have an exit strategy. Founders eventually retire and younger generations are not always interested in moving into the family business. For services businesses, valuations tend to rely on productivity, which can be hard to predict when you're providing discrete project based services. Many times when services businesses are acquired, they are being bought for the people. Conversely, the value in a Cloud ERP business is in the future revenue streams associated with the customer base, which tends to be stable, especially through the lens of a historical track record. What this means is to the extent you can successfully transition your business to Cloud ERP, you will affect a stable, predictable business model that will provide for a profitable exit strategy

Chapter

6

Questions about my customer

You can please some of the people all of the time and all of the people some of the time, but you can't please all of the people all of the time.

John Lydgate (English Poet, c.1370 – c.1451)

B
UILDING it does not mean they will come!!! Getting inside your customers head will be a crucial step in ensuring that you get your Cloud ERP offer right.

Simply replicating your current on-premises offer runs the risk of failing to address the "new normal" business challenges that have driven your customers to consider the Cloud in the first place.

6.1 What is their cloud motivation

At a basic level there needs to be something that is motivating your customer to consider the Cloud. If there is not or you are not able to tap into the motivations that do exist then you may have a tough time convincing customers to change from what they have today.

It is also important to recognize the anti-motivations that will act as blockers within an organization. Blockers typically attract a higher weighting and so the benefits you provide need to do more than just compensate.

☒	Question	Why this matters
☐	6.1.1 How did your customers perform through the economic crisis?	The economic crisis has been difficult for everyone and, for many businesses, proved fatal. One of the attractive things about Cloud ERP is it typically requires limited startup costs, scales based on need, and does not require a long term contract. For your customers who are looking at IT systems that may not have not been maintained or upgraded to save costs, Cloud ERP may create an opportunity to reduce the upfront cost and risk associated with IT spend
☐	6.1.2 How innovative are your customers?	Customers involved in innovative segments or who have dynamic business models in conservative niches are likely to be early adopters of Cloud ERP. These customers will be more willing to take the perceived risk associated with moving IT to the Cloud than customers who are involved in conservative industries
☐	6.1.3 Are your customers transforming business operations / processes?	First, if you know whether your customers are transforming business operations / processes or not, it says a lot about your relationships and the long term prospects of your organization. Organizations that are undergoing business transformation may be looking for Cloud ERP solutions that are informed by best practices. Adopting a Cloud ERP solution signals the intent to truly transform. To the extent business processes are aligned with Cloud ERP, this makes integration and change management simpler, which means faster time to value and better ROI

☒	Question	Why this matters
☐	6.1.4 Are your customers' IT shops in crisis?	IT frequently has a hard time demonstrating to the business that they provide value. When times are good, IT shops can rely on a certain amount of opacity and the implied business risk associated with disaster scenarios. However, when times are bad, CIOs are sometimes given a mandate to achieve across the board cost reductions and IT projects that have overrun come under scrutiny. For IT shops in crisis, Cloud ERP may represent a way to reduce costs and shift some of the IT burden to an external vendor. This will be welcomed relief for CIOs whose IT shops are on fire
☐	6.1.5 How invested in traditional ERP are your customers?	Sunk costs arguments are typically lost on IT shops that have made significant, and often painful, investments in traditional ERP. Decisions about Cloud ERP may be more emotional than rationale. Understanding that a new Cloud ERP solution, regardless of how elegant, may not be welcome in an organization that just completed an 18 month traditional ERP implementation is critical
☐	6.1.6 How painful is traditional ERP for your customers?	Customers that never quite got their traditional ERP system to work or are reliant on a legacy system that has not been recently updated or upgraded may be interested in Cloud ERP. For many of these customers the notion of shutting down the old system and turning on something new that does not require a lot of time to customize or implement will be attractive

☒	Question	Why this matters
☐	6.1.7 Would Cloud ERP accelerate time to value for your customers?	A common complaint for traditional ERP has been long, disruptive implementations where benefits tend to get lost or are unrealized. The Cloud ERP concept of a solution that requires minimal configuration and can be efficiently scaled up and down promises to dramatically accelerate time to value. With Cloud ERP, years and months become weeks and days
☐	6.1.8 Do your customers have decentralized business operations?	In the initial phases of Cloud ERP adoption as solutions mature, two-tier ERP systems are attractive to customers. Two-tier ERP typically means that headquarter and mission critical business processes are supported by the traditional ERP with non-mission critical business processes and branch offices running Cloud ERP solutions
☐	6.1.9 Do your customers have extensive HR resources?	ERP workloads are experiencing different adoption rates in the Cloud with HR leading the way. To the extent your customers have extensive HR departments, Cloud ERP solutions are likely to be attractive

☒	**Question**	**Why this matters**
☐	6.1.10 Are there legal / regulatory issues that impact your customers' ability to adopt Cloud solutions?	Industries have different legal / regulatory issues, which impact things like where data can reside and the traceability and transparency associated with various business processes. In some cases, legal / regulatory requirements may be minimal. For example, manufacturing is an early adopter of Cloud, partially because there are few restrictions in terms of where data can reside. Conversely, Federal governments are particularly sensitive to where data resides. Additionally, there are geographic considerations. So, for example, Europe tends to have more regulations around how data is stored and used than the APAC. Understanding how industry and geographic legal / regulatory issues are likely to impact the ability of your customers to adopt Cloud ERP so you can suggest a solution that works for their business is critical

6.2 Questions about their business

Being clear about the underlying business processes and dynamics of your customer will help you provide a secondary layer to your offer that compliments your understanding of their motivations.

You will have additional information that allows you to further clarify the focus and messaging of the offer you are proposing.

Crucially you will be able to maximize the benefits that a Cloud approach can offer OR realize at an early stage that a Cloud offer may be too difficult to sell to this customer at this time.

☒ Question	Why this matters
☐ 6.2.1 Which verticals do your customers do business in?	Adoption of Cloud ERP varies by industry. Typically, manufacturing, financial services, and general services lead followed by the public sector. To the extent your customers sit in verticals that are early adopters, you will need to accelerate the transition to Cloud ERP
☐ 6.2.2 How involved is the business in IT decisions?	Because Cloud typically represents the simplification of IT for end users, the business tends to get more involved in decisions that used to be the sole domain of IT. This varies by industry and geography, but regardless, there is a clear trend for the business to be more involved in IT decisions as Cloud accelerates. This dynamic is positive for Cloud ERP. In many cases, the business may have already trialed a Cloud application and then come to IT for support. To the extent business stakeholders at your customers are actively involved in IT decisions, this will create Cloud ERP opportunities
☐ 6.2.3 Do you have relationships outside the IT shop?	As business becomes increasingly involved in IT decision, you will need to increasingly interact with and sell to the business and your ability to develop deep relationships with both the business and IT stakeholders is key to long term success
☐ 6.2.4 How much do you know about your customers' vertical IT processes?	A deep understanding of your customers vertical IT processes allows you to recommend hybrid solutions where vertically specific IT processes are delivered via traditional ERP and horizontal processes are delivered by the Cloud. This means that you can suggest a solution that optimizes benefits because it is unique to your customer's need. In turn, this leads to the deep relationships that are critical as Cloud matures

☒	Question	Why this matters
☐	6.2.5 How much do you know about your customers' vertical business processes?	Vertical business expertise is critical in the transition to Cloud ERP. It allows you to build deep relationships with both IT and the business and it creates opportunities to provide additional business process related services to your customers, which positions you as a trusted advisor and compensates for the erosion in traditional development and integration
☐	6.2.6 How asset intensive is the business?	Customers with asset intensive business models tend to think in terms of CapEx, which includes IT. It may be harder for these customers to adopt the OpEx mentality that describes Cloud ERP
☐	6.2.7 Are your customers good at change management?	In traditional ERP implementations, change management tends to focus on user adoption. For Cloud ERP, this definition needs to be expanded to include IT and business processes. Cloud ERP represents the outsourcing of complexity that was a form of job security for the IT shop. In order for vendors to manage this complexity, Cloud ERP solutions are designed to be configured, but not customized. The outcomes of this dynamic is change management that may force the business to make minor adjustments to business processes to align with Cloud ERP and IT shops that may have to reexamine what they do for a living. This is likely to be disruptive and your ability to help customers understand the change management impact of Cloud ERP is important

☒	Question	Why this matters
☐	6.2.8 Are your customer's workforces comprised of knowledge workers?	Knowledge workers expect to work in high performance workplaces, characterized by cutting edge applications and active collaboration. These expectations are frequently upset when workers confront the reality of trying to figure out how to use a highly customized legacy ERP solution that is closer to a green screen DOS experience than using an iPhone. Cloud ERP tends to be more aligned with the workplace knowledge workers expect and your customers who have large knowledge workforces will be early adopters
☐	6.2.9 How technically adept is the leadership team?	Management tends to set the tone for the way businesses look at and think about technology. To the extent your customers' leadership teams are active consumers of the latest greatest technology, they are likely to be interested in Cloud ERP
☐	6.2.10 How are IT purchase decisions made?	The IT buying center is complex and, in the Cloud, this will increase as the business becomes more involved. Effectively selling Cloud ERP requires a detailed understanding of not just the ultimate decision maker, but the influencers and censors that impact a buy decision. In the early stages of the shift to Cloud, a key influencer might be the CEO who saw something in the media about Cloud ERP or the CFO who read about some interesting functionality online. These stakeholders might be behind the scenes with the power to say no. Understanding both the business and IT stakeholders in a Cloud ERP buy decision is critical

☒	**Question**	**Why this matters**
☐	6.2.11 Do your customers have distributed offices?	Cloud services have been shown to be especially appealing to organizations with a distributed physical setup. They will typically have a complex technology infrastructure that they want to simplify. Also all but those in the "head Office" will be used to access services remotely.
☐	6.2.12 Is there a high level of mobile workforce?	Mobile workers are often disenfranchised from on-premises ERP offerings. Cloud deployments are inherently friendlier to these user types.
☐	6.2.13 Is your customer in a highly regulated market?	Although many of the issues raised about security, data location, data sovereignty etc. in highly regulated industries can be addressed it does leave you potentially open to complexities both during the sales process and after deployment. The ongoing efforts by vendors, governments and the marketplace in general will help to address these over time. So it may be prudent to consider whether these business areas should be part of your initial sales focus.

6.3 Technology

Whilst the focus of your offer is likely to be around a business based value proposition, it is not prudent to ignore the technology aspects of your customer. The customers approach to technology and their recent deployments

and investment could be either supportive of your offer, or a major blocker. It is unlikely that the CFO is going to be supportive or impressed with a proposal for a "rip and replace" Cloud ERP solution when the business has recently spent $$$$ on an on-premises upgrade. However a Hybrid offering that allows currently disenfranchised users to fully participate through the extension of the current environment via a Cloud offering may be seen more favorably.

☒	Question	Why this matters
☐	6.3.1 Have your customers recently deployed Cloud solutions?	The best indicator of a desire to use Cloud solutions is current use. Talking to your customers about the sum total of their IT plans allows you to understand potential drivers of interest in Cloud ERP. For example, customers who have recently implemented Private Cloud infrastructure may want to lift their legacy ERP into the Cloud. This is the perfect opportunity to talk about Cloud ERP
☐	6.3.2 How sophisticated are your customers' IT shops?	While Cloud represents the simplification of IT for users, in the early stages of adoption it is sometimes simpler for sophisticated IT shops to evaluate the risks and rewards associated with Cloud. One way to think about this is to consider that customers likely to adopt Cloud ERP are either sophisticated businesses that can clearly evaluate risks and rewards or simple businesses that have not typically invested in complex IT. It is the customers who are in the middle, who are unable to consider how Cloud could impact their IT operations, that are most likely to want to defend the legacy IT strategy
☐	6.3.3 How robust is your customers' infrastructure?	One of the top complaints associated with Cloud applications (including ERP) is latency associated with poor network infrastructure. Being able to access a Cloud ERP solution is convenient, but not if access is slow or spotty because your customers' network infrastructure is outdated. Recommending a solution based on your customers' current infrastructure limits the disappointment associated with investing in a new technology and not having it work

☒	Question	Why this matters
☐	6.3.4 What percentage of revenue do your customers devote to IT?	In the same way that Cloud is attractive to either highly sophisticated or simple IT shops, Cloud ERP is likely to appeal to customers that devote a large percentage of revenue to IT and customers that spend little. This will correlate with sophisticated and simple IT shops who will see value in Cloud ERP, although for different reasons. It is the customers in the middle who will be less likely to invest in Cloud ERP in the early stages of adoption
☐	6.3.5 Have your customers recently invested in traditional ERP?	While sunk cost arguments should prevail in how your customers think about IT, the reality is investments in traditional ERP are both emotional and financial. An organization that has made a significant commitment to investing in traditional ERP is unlikely to consider a Cloud ERP solution
☐	6.3.6 Are your customers running the most recent version of their traditional ERP?	Falling behind on the ERP upgrade cycle can signal financial distress, fear of change, or simple apathy. And while running the latest instance of an ERP solution is not always required, the further behind a customer gets the larger the gap between their current ERP application and best of breed solutions. As the gap grows, customers increasingly wonder if Cloud ERP will allow them to bypass a painful upgrade. This creates a perfect opportunity to talk to them about Cloud ERP

☒ Question	Why this matters
6.3.7 How customized are your customers' traditional ERP?	Traditionally, ERP customization is driven by one of two forces. Sometimes vendors, in an attempt to increase revenue, convince customers they need to customize the solution or the customer actually needs to customize the ERP solution because they have a unique business processes. There is a lot of evidence that suggests that customers are growing tired of the cost associated with highly customized ERP solutions, which bodes well for Cloud ERP that is configurable. To the extent your customer's ERP solution was customized because of an overzealous vendor, they will be a good candidate for Cloud ERP
6.3.8 How often do your customers' refresh their application portfolios?	Customers that continually refresh their application portfolios are likely to be tired of the costs associated with upgrading, maintaining, and making sure applications work together to support business performance. These customers will be interested in working with Cloud vendors that can provide integrated solutions where many of the integration issues become the responsibility of the vendor
6.3.9 How concerned are your customers about data security?	There are many reasons customers are concerned about data security. Sometimes it has to do with legal / regulatory issues. Sometimes it is an emotional reaction based on a personal experience. Understanding your customers' perspective on data security and what that means for Cloud ERP is critical to building profitable relationships

☒	Question	Why this matters
☐	6.3.10 Have your customers experienced IT issues that negatively impacted the business?	The reality is the simple costs associated with negative IT issues create significant drag on the business. To the extent that the issue was related to traditional, on-premises IT, like an ERP implementation that went significantly over budget or failed to realize the predicted benefits, then this is likely to increase interest in Cloud ERP. On the other hand, to the extent the issue was related to the Cloud like an outage or loss of data, then this is likely to decrease interest in Cloud ERP. Understanding the depth and impact of negative IT issues allows you to help your customers invest in IT solutions that avoid the sins of the past

Chapter

7

Questions for vendors

Assumptions are the termites of relationships.

Henry Winkler (American Actor, 1945 –)

Y OU are committed and are clear about the customers that you can put a compelling offer in front of. You have years of experience and are familiar with the current on-premises ecosystem and vendor capability. However you are about to make a move to a new Cloud based model.

Are the current "best" vendors providing credible Cloud propositions? Have they slipped behind or are they timing their entry just right? The startups may look interesting, but do they have the track record that will provide confidence to your customers in what is traditional a conservative area of business solutions?

The "outsourcing" aspect of the Cloud model is one of its benefits, however it also raises concerns about loss of control, quality of services etc. Asking questions of your vendors will satisfy your concerns and provide you with the confidence to address these concerns with your customers.

7.1 Capability

Having a good idea is only the starting point of delivering a solution. The skills required will cover multiple disciplines and the costs can be significant.

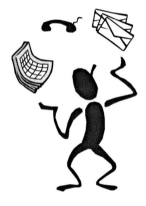

This is true even for relatively simple offerings, however when we consider ERP, especially in the mid to enterprise market, this is multiplied by many magnitudes. Now layer onto this the new requirements in a Cloud world and we grow the requirements even further.

Making sure your vendor has the correct capabilities will be an important part of your due diligence.

☒	Question	Why this matters
☐	7.1.1 Does your Cloud ERP vendor have global sales / marketing?	With every emerging technology that promises transformation comes a raft of vendors that promise to have the best technology. While a superior solution is important, it is also important that your vendor have the kind of global sales / marketing support where they can actively help you generate and realize demand as well as create opportunities for you to monetize vertical applications built from your expertise
☐	7.1.2 Is your Cloud ERP vendor good at selling online?	While Cloud ERP solutions imply a certain amount of complexity, Cloud solutions in general are an online phenomena. This means Cloud ERP enables online sales, marketing, and fulfillment. However, not every vendor is good at selling online or is willing to make the investment required to develop these competencies
☐	7.1.3 Does your Cloud ERP vendor have global data center infrastructure?	When the data center providing a Cloud ERP solution goes down, customer screens literally go blank. These disruptions can have a negative impact on customer businesses and vendor brands. You should make sure that your Cloud ERP vendor has the requisite data center coverage to support your customers and you should also make sure that the potential negative impact to your vendor's brand creates a powerful incentive to maintain the infrastructure and assure customer access to Cloud ERP. A startup with nothing to lose will take risks that a large vendor with other assets to protect will not.

☒	Question	Why this matters
☐	7.1.4 Has your Cloud ERP vendor experienced significant outages?	Even the most robust infrastructure can experience technical issues. Having said that, sometimes outages speak to cultural issues where root problems remain unaddressed so the issues continue. Outages happen, but you should consider how your Cloud ERP vendor addressed the problem, how they communicated with your customers and the extent to which the problem is endemic or a one off with a logical explanation
☐	7.1.5 Does your Cloud ERP vendor invest in vertical solutions?	This is a two edged sword. To the extent you have significant vertical expertise and have developed proprietary solutions, the last thing in the world you want to do is compete with your vendor. On the other hand, to the extent you rely on your vendor to provide vertical solutions, then you want them to invest. There is no right answer, but to the extent your vendor provides vertical solutions and captures the associated revenue then you run the risk of getting pushed into a commodity business where the vendor looks to you to generate demand and provide simple configuration services
☐	7.1.6 Does your Cloud ERP vendor provide a development platform?	Developing vertical Cloud ERP applications requires a development platform. To the extent the platform provides a familiar development environment like Microsoft Azure if you are a .Net shop, then it will be much simpler for you to build Cloud ERP applications. To the extent the development platform is integrated with other solutions like an application marketplace, then your vertical expertise will be simpler to monetize

☒ Question	Why this matters
☐ 7.1.7 Does your Cloud ERP vendor provide a Cloud ERP application marketplace?	An application marketplace provides a transaction platform where you can sell vertical applications globally. Many Cloud application vendors have marketplaces. What you need to determine is to what extent is the application marketplace a thriving market that creates an opportunity versus a pretty storefront with no customers
☐ 7.1.8 Does your Cloud ERP vendor have global support resources?	As your Cloud ERP business grows and you sell applications in new geographies, you will need a vendor who can support you on a global basis. It is one thing to be able to sell an application you developed to the far reaches of the world, but the same technology that enables global distribution provides a voice for unhappy customers, which can have a negative impact on your business in your core geographies
☐ 7.1.9 Does your Cloud ERP solution cover multiple workloads?	Cloud ERP adoption is being driven by HR and finance. So, at a minimum, your vendor needs to be able to support these workloads. To the extent your vendor also supports manufacturing and operations and asset management, then they are likely to be more relevant to your customers
☐ 7.1.10 Does your Cloud ERP vendor offer other Cloud solutions?	Cloud ERP is likely to lead in the sense that customers that buy Cloud ERP solutions tend to be interested in additional Cloud solutions. The ability of your Cloud vendor to provide a complete stack of applications makes you more relevant to your customers and creates opportunities for you to get a better return on your sales and marketing investments

7.2 Credibility

Any decision regarding a company's ERP systems is typically taken very seriously. There is a reputation for more conservative thinking, which is probably a good thing – it is OK for the sales staff to be "creative" but we need to know that the money is being looked after.

No matter how good the benefits of a Cloud ERP offer might be, there will be an understandable concern about trusting something as important as ERP to something new like the Cloud.

A key aspect about addressing these concerns will be both your credibility and that of the vendor that is providing the underlying service.

☒ Question	Why this matters
☐ 7.2.1 Has your vendor made a significant brand investment in Cloud?	Vendors who have made a significant public commitment to Cloud have a lot to lose if they fall down providing Cloud ERP. Not only will they be negatively perceived in the Cloud, but there legacy technology positioning is also likely to suffer. In a sense, these vendors have 'burned the ships' in their commitment to Cloud and, thus, failure is not an option
☐ 7.2.2 Does your vendor have a clear Cloud vision?	With all the hype, some vendors have publically announced that they are in the Cloud, but lack a clear vision that describes what Cloud means for their partners and customers. These vendors may not be serious about the Cloud. Conversely, vendors who have a clear vision with real investments and progress in terms of solutions that can clearly describe why their partners and customers should care are serious about the Cloud. These are the vendors you should considering aligning with
☐ 7.2.3 Has your vendor announced their Cloud vision to the market?	It is one thing to float your cloud strategy by internal stakeholder and partners to gauge their reaction. It is something else to talk publically about Cloud aspirations. When vendors announce to the market that they intend to provide Cloud ERP, they are creating a standard that will be used to measure their progress and signaling their commitment to reaching their goals
☐ 7.2.4 Does your vendor have a history of providing effective solutions?	The extent to which your vendor has a reputation for providing effective solutions, robust support, and active investments in partner success is a sign that they are likely to be a good Cloud ERP partner

☒	Question	Why this matters
☐	7.2.5 Is your vendor willing to 'make it right' when something goes wrong?	As with any new technology, things inevitably go wrong. Recent outages at Amazon and Sony attest to the reality that regardless of how technically adept your vendor is, bad things can happen. And while consistent outages are a bad sign, a vendor's ability to recognize and effectively remediate issues says a lot about their commitment to you and your customers' success
☐	7.2.6 Does your vendor have the financial resources to withstand market turbulence?	The Cloud has spawned a range of startups looking to capitalize on the Cloud promise of transformation. Some of these organizations will thrive, but many will not. To the extent your Cloud vendor may not have the financial resources to survive as a going concern and invest in your success then, regardless of how good their Cloud ERP solution seems, tying your success to theirs creates risk for your long term business prospects
☐	7.2.7 What is the media saying about your vendor's Cloud ERP solution?	The media can be fickle and, in a world where anyone with access to the internet can voice their opinions on a global scale, you need to be careful about sources of information. It is relatively simple to set up a news alert with keywords that will catch vendor announcements about Cloud ERP and media reaction. To the extent that there is a consistent flow of coordinated announcements coming from your vendor and the media reaction is generally positive, this is a good sign that your vendor will make a good long term partner

☒ **Question**	**Why this matters**
☐ 7.2.8 What are industry analysts saying about your vendors Cloud ERP solution?	Industry analysts make a living by thinking about technology vendors and customers. They will be privy to information provided directly by the vendor and the reactions of customers. To the extent these analysts are part of a reputable firm like IDC or Gartner then they are likely to be accurate. If analysts have a positive reaction to a vendor's Cloud ERP solution then this suggests they will be a good partner
☐ 7.2.9 What are partners / customers saying about your vendors Cloud ERP solution?	Perhaps the best indication of the viability of your vendor's Cloud ERP solution is what partners and customers are saying. These constituents' businesses will rely on Cloud ERP and to the extent they have positive things to say, it means your vendor has a valuable solution
☐ 7.2.10 Can your vendor fully embrace Cloud ERP solutions?	Some vendors have a substantial investment in traditional on-premises ERP solutions. This investment may make it difficult to embrace the Cloud, which represents a radical departure from the business model that has made these vendors successful. Said vendors may provide Cloud ERP solutions but not be serious about promoting and investing in their success

7.3 Commitment

A vendor may have the capability and resources to deliver a Cloud offering. They may have credibility both from their historical track record and the announcements they have made about their cloud plans.

 However the ERP market has a longer investment cycle than many other areas of IT with systems once implemented being retained for 5 or more years. Has the vendor got the commitment to work through the many technical and commercial challenges that will inevitably come their way as the Cloud market matures?

This is not just about addressing concerns that your customers may raise, but also about giving you the confidence to make what is likely to be a big bet within your own business.

☒ Question	Why this matters
☐ 7.3.1 Is your vendor actively investing in Cloud ERP solutions?	Cloud ERP investment can take many forms, all of which are important. Obviously, a viable Cloud ERP solution is critical. Additionally, active investments in sales and marketing, partner programs, events, Cloud development platforms, application marketplaces, and a complete Cloud application stack are all signs that your vendor is serious about the Cloud
☐ 7.3.2 Is your vendor actively investing in Cloud ERP partner programs?	Partner programs include everything from the mechanics of revenue splits to active sales and marketing support. The key issue here is to the extent to which your Cloud ERP vendor is truly committed to partner success, which means clarifying roles and responsibilities and an active commitment to creating opportunities for you to grow your business without having to compete with your vendor
☐ 7.3.3 Does your vendor provide sales / marketing support?	As the business becomes involved in Cloud ERP decisions, the ability of your vendor to provide sales and marketing support becomes increasingly important. Your vendor's commitment to providing coordinated offline sales and marketing support where you do not, for example, coordinating to make sure you do not compete with them in key word auctions for search engine marketing is important. Vendors that are willing to provide offline resources like executives or sales support to help you close large deals are committed to your success

☒	Question	Why this matters
☐	7.3.4 Does your vendor provide leads?	The relationship between Cloud and the internet means effective online demand generation. To the extent your vendor can generate leads and distribute them equitably, then you can invest less in demand generation and focus on closing sales and developing relationships
☐	7.3.5 Is your vendor actively 'selling' you on Cloud ERP?	There is a fine line between overselling Cloud ERP and actively investing in making sure you understand the vendor strategy, associated value proposition, and your role. There should be a tight linkage between the promises your vendor makes and how they deliver
☐	7.3.6 Is your vendor willing to invest in your organization?	Making the transition to Cloud ERP is likely to be turbulent and, for many partners, active vendor support will be critical to long term success. Vendors can support your organization directly by financing contracts or indirectly by investing in general marketing campaigns. The best vendor for you is the one that offers a wide range of support where your commitment is repaid by an active investment in your long-term success
☐	7.3.7 Is your vendor's partner revenue split equitable?	With Cloud ERP, the way you divvy up annuity revenue streams forms the foundation of your Cloud business model. The most effective revenue splits lead to short term cash flow and long term sustainability. You should be wary of vendors that emphasize upfront payments at the cost of long-term revenue or vice versa

☒	Question	Why this matters
☐	7.3.8 Does your vendor have clear rules of engagement?	One of the common concerns for Cloud partners is in a future where vendors deliver IT directly to customers, partners become irrelevant. This concern is valid, but can be addressed by vendors who have a historical commitment to partners based on rules of engagement with clearly defined roles and responsibilities that create headroom for partners to profit
☐	7.3.9 Do you compete with your vendor?	The extent to which your partner provides vertical applications or services can create conflicts of interest and competition. What you should look for is historical trends and current / future investments. If your vendor is actively investing in vertical R&D for their Cloud ERP solution or building out their services organization, then you may be increasingly competing with them
☐	7.3.10 Does your vendor provide adequate headroom on the wholesale Cloud ERP cost for you to be profitable?	Vendors that are committed to your success will provide Cloud ERP at a wholesale price that leaves room for you to wrap additional services around the solution and be competitive with other Cloud ERP solutions. At the same time, the wholesale price that impacts your annuity revenue stream needs to be seen through the lens of the full set of opportunities your vendor provides for you to be profitable, which includes things like a development platform and an application marketplace

☒ Question	Why this matters
☐ 7.3.11 Does your vendor rely on you to develop vertical IP?	A critical component of your value proposition to vendors is your ability to provide vertical IP. Cloud ERP vendors understand that your ability to put feet on the street, to interact with business and IT executives in your target markets, and to develop vertical specific applications that make the vendor Cloud ERP solution more relevant to customers is critical to their long term success. It is also a form of job security in your Cloud ERP vendor relationship and insurance against becoming an undifferentiated commodity service provider

Chapter

8

Call to Action

A conclusion is the place where you got tired of thinking.

Albert Bloch (American Artist, 1882 – 1961)

UNDERSTAND that any shift to a diversified business strategy requires investment, focus, and reprioritization. Take the time to identify where your business requires the most attention and make the commitment to drive this evolution to increase your opportunity to develop long term annuity streams and brand differentiation for your company:

- Assess your readiness
- Invest in business & technical resources dedicated to cloud based sales and solutions
- Start with what you know and leverage your existing customer base to enhance what you can offer those customers today
- Lead through innovation by developing industry relevant, packaged solutions that are readily consumable
- Prioritize web-based, nurture marketing to drive demand generation and rethink your cost of goods sold

It will take time for any organization to build the right business model to support the ever changing demands of a cloud based business. Take the time to plan effectively and develop a blueprint that best serves the optimal market opportunity for your company and the capabilities you have to offer.

Resources

You may find the following resources and useful as part of your own ongoing research:

- The Microsoft Dynamics Cloud Partner Profitability Guide (*https://partner.microsoft.com/global/productssolutions/40162698*)
- Microsoft Cloud Power home page (*http://www.microsoft.com/cloud/default.aspx*)
- Microsoft Online Services Team Blog (*http://blogs.technet.com/b/msonline/*)
- Microsoft Online Services LinkedIn group (*http://www.linkedin.com/groups/Microsoft-Online-Services-1789204*)
- National Institute of Standards and Technology – Cloud Computing (*http://www.nist.gov/itl/cloud/index.cfm*)
- Microsoft announce ERP in the cloud plans (*http://www.cio.com/article/679360/Microsoft_Putting_ERP_in_the_Azure_Cloud*)
- Microsoft Partner Network Dynamics ERP pages (*https://partner.microsoft.com/global/productssolutions/dynamics/dynamicserp*)

Notes pages

Please use these notes pages to scribble your doodles and map out your thoughts.

Notes pages

9 781907 453090